An Alchemy
of
Musings

Dr. Vandita Dharni

TGIBT PRESS

Published by "**The Great Indian Book Tour**"
Imprint : **T G I B T   P r e s s**
www.tgibt.com
email : prashant@tgibt.com

Title : **An Alchemy of Musings**
Author : Vandita Dharni
Copyright © Vandita Dharni 2022
All rights reserved

First published in 2022
First Edition 2022

ISBN : 978-93-93262-14-1

All rights reserved. No part of this book can be used, reproduced in any manner whatsoever without written permission from the author, except in the case of brief quotations embodied in articles or reviews.

CONTENTS

Introduction   1
Preface   6
Acknowledgments   10

A) POEMS

1. A Ballet of Life   13
2. A Familiar Tap   14
3. Caught Between Hemispheres   15
4. In the Heart of the Forest   16
5. Catamaran Dreams   18
6. An Enigma   19
7. Aphrodite   20
8. Life Gives Us a Second Chance   21
9. Crossroads of Life   22
10. Shards of Love   23
11. Reignited Hopes   24
12. The Clairvoyant's Cigar   25
13. The Haven I Yearn For   26
14. Utopia   27
15. Waxen Musings   28
16. Whimsical Ink   29
17. The Lost Sonnet   31
18. My Paradise   32
19. Sweet Poison   34
20. The Weeds   36

21. The Mangled Womb   38

22. Solitude   39

23. Childhood Deconstructed   40

24. A Eunoia   41

25. How to Make   42

26. Disinheritance   44

27. A Language Unknown   45

28. Silence   47

29. Poetry Misunderstood   49

30. A Furry Encounter   53

31. Feuille Morte   55

32. Residue of Memories   56

33. Eight O' Clock   57

34. Soirees   58

35. The Love Affair   59

36. A New Dawn   61

37. Those Red Tulips   62

38. My Roots   63

39. In the Still of the Night   65

40. My Identity My Name   67

41. The Mist   68

42. Nature's Gem   69

43. Eerie Encounters   70

44. Déjà vu   71

45. The Tree with A Familiar Scent   72

46. The Enchantress   73

47. Bonhomie   74

48. A Lost Cause 75
49. The Montage 76
50. Non-Existent Identity 77
51. Showers of Love 79
52. The Treacherous Mandrel 80
53. A New Identity 81
54. An Autumnal Night 83
55. The Birth of a Poem 84
56. Waiting 85
57. Time's Filigree 87
58. Carpe Diem 88
59. Still Familiar 89
60. My Own Story 91
61. A Tribute to Mother Ganges 93
62. Let's Play a Game 95
63. A Haibun: Monsters Under the Bed 97
64. The Lazy Music Sings 98
65. A Metamorphosis 100
66. When the Angels Danced on their Heads 102
67. Dead Silences 103
68. Grey Clouds 104

B) ROSEATE SONNETS

(A form that is pioneered by Dr. Koshy A.V.)

69. The Ice Maiden 105
70. The Science of Not Knowing 106

71. Blue Roses   107

72. The Snow Girl   108

73. The River   109

74. Wheatfield with Crows   110

75. Eau de Vie Nights   111

C) PROSE POEMS

76. Crimson Hues   112

77. A Foofaraw   113

78. Summer Escapades   114

79. A War Veteran's Story   115

80. The Menagerie   116

INTRODUCTION

Vandita Dharni, in her own write/right, "is a published poet and hails from an eminent family of educationists. She currently resides in Chandigarh, India. She has earned many a distinction in the literary field, however in her academic pursuits she raised the bar by topping the University of Allahabad at the post-graduate level in English. Thereafter, she earned a Ph.D. degree in American Literature from the same university.

She has submitted articles, poems and short stories that have been published in journals such as Criterion, Ruminations, GNOSIS, HellBound Publishing House, Borderless journal, RIC journal and International e-zines like Immagine and Poessia, Synchronised Chaos, Guido Gozzano, Silver Birch Press, Raven Cage, SETU, Fasihi magazine, TSL Roseate Sonnets Anthology, Our Poetry Archive, Primer Antologia De Poetas Del Proyecto De Unamos Al Mundo Con La Poesia- Mexico, Poleart, Albania and Inner Child Press, U.S.A.

Her dream achieved fruition when she published three solo anthologies, Quintessential Outpourings, The Oyster of Love and Rippling Overtures within a span of four years. Her latest contributions include the Roseate Sonnet Anthology and Breathe Poetry anthology. She has co- edited anthologies such as 'The Petals of Peace' and 'The Ruddy Ravens, Cheshire Cats and Rusty Rats' to name a few. She has also reviewed several poems on poetry sites such as Cultural Reverence and 'Poetry Review' on Facebook.

She has been honoured with the Poetic Galaxy Award 2018 by the Literati Cosmos Society, the World Poetic Star award

2019 by the World Nation's Writers' Union, and several others. She is also an administrator for How to Write for Success Literary Forum and Literary Criticism and theory."

An Alchemy of Musings is her fourth collection of poems. Reading it was quite an experience. It contains eighty poems divided into three sections, the first being the meatiest offering, the second one a tribute to my altered form of the sonnet, the roseate sonnet, which makes me cock-a-whoop with joy, the third being a section of prose poems. Vandita is, like me, a poet who asks for much from the reader. She is learned, allusive, inter-textual and referential and to understand her poems completely expects you to do some spadework and research. It will pay you off well to do it, I assure you. To illustrate what I told you, her very first poem in the collection 'A Ballet of Life' refers to the Nutcracker Suite by Tchaikovsky which comes to us here at one remove through her reference to the Nutcracker movie. The success of a good poem, it is said, is that even if it refers to something outside the ken of the reader making it slightly cerebral or intellectual, it should still work as a poem and connect with the audience even if they don't get these allusions and here Vandita does it. We are mesmerised by her vocabulary and her diction in which she also mixes in words uncommon and from languages like French but most of all by an essential simplicity in the poem which underlies its outward complexity and draws us in to let it speak to our hearts. The poem also has a structure and wisdom older than the hills as it moves from "there is more value in evil than brocade" to "there is no value in evil than brocade." It is instructive. It is poetic. Vandita gives us all we look for in poems, in poem after poem, and it is obvious she is both conscious about what she is doing and doing it well, which is different from the general run of the mill poems one gets to read these days.

Indian English poetry has many good women writers these days like Vandita Dharni. and I was reminded of my reading of poets roughly the same age as her probably, in their thirties and forties, like Mandakini Pachauri, Rukhaya MK, Sophia Naz, Deepika KC Chand, Zeenath Ibrahim, Jagari Mukherjee, Rochelle Potkar, Sufia Khatoon, Vineetha Mekkoth, Reena Prasad, and others who all write with the same kind of intensity or finesse, all from India or in India and all writing in English. This is a very rich vein and will hopefully be tapped by readers accordingly, abundantly, in terms of reading pleasure and enjoyment.

To return to Vandita's collection, her very titles are worth study as they give away her themes and she is modern in using spacing in some of her poems. Writing roseate sonnets shows she can write in form and her prose poems are marvellous reading. She has also got a haibun in there and many of these poems were written to prompts in TSL's Napowrimo showing she can write from the heart as well as to order.

One of my favourites due to its reference to the famous Wheatfield with Crows painting by Vincent van Gogh is her roseate sonnet inspired by it.

Wheatfield with Crows
(Inspired from a painting by Van Gogh)

Come golden spring, fields smear streaks
of mosaic tapestry, charcoaled wings immerse
their brows of grief in sodden straw heads waving,
shrugging the silver scythe hanging in the blue overhead.

Those harbingers swoop brazenly stringing
ominous secrets, pollinating death but hope still glistens
on goldfish backs against cobalt wrinkles- a night's embers
Parrot ribbons smoulder in fire, tongues lashing them.

Leopards run amok in gold flecked catharsis
mulling over this legerity in its caryopsis.

Ripened grain's endless fissures, embracing,
Outsourcing colours from bleeding palettes,
Squawking crows canvassed into ebony clusters
Etching an impasto of sustained hopelessness.

The poem appealed to me as ekphrastic and not just in flattering me by its choice of form but what really impressed me in it is the honest response to Van Gogh's work summed up in the last word "hopelessness." Here too we see a semi-circle in the poem from "hope" to "hopelessness" and whether I or van Gogh agree begs the question, as what matters is the rich attempt to portray the inner feelings of the poet in question to the artist's work. Rich is perhaps the best adjective to describe Vandita's poetry and her aesthetics as reflected in its world.

The prose poems are littered with gems: "Snowflakes of mind's nightfall melt away leaving a phlegmatic silence on puckered lips. Its frayed edges hurt the skin like brambles on a storm-tossed day. 'Somewhere my Love' jars in my ears, stinging them with deceit that lingers like an aftertaste in my mouth as I guzzle down Maraschino liqueur. The rawness of guilt haunts me as I succumb to the craving yet again. The candle burns out as its wax melts away. This foofaraw in a capricious butterfly's life isn't so simple after all."

What did I say? rich. Rich. RICH. Thanks for having enriched me, Vandita. All the best to you and these eighty poems as they set out on their own journey to their readers. May the best ones, the ones meant to find them, their kindred souls, find them. All the best always, dear co-editor of Ruddy Ravens, Cheshire Cats and Rusty Rats.

Dr. Ampat Varghese Koshy

Dr. Koshy A.V. has till recently been working as an Assistant Professor in the English Department of Jazan University, Saudi Arabia. He has many books, degrees, diplomas, certificates, prizes, and awards to his credit and also, besides teaching, is an editor, anthology maker, poet, critic and writer of fiction. He runs an autism NPO with his wife, Anna Gabriel. Two of his co-authored books published in 2020 were Amazon best-sellers in India and USA, namely, 'Wine-kissed Poems' with Jagari Mukherjee and 'Vodka by the Volga' with Dr. Santosh Bakaya. His latest achievements are winning a prestigious certificate in Italy for his poetry and working as Visiting Professor in FET, Jain University, Bangalore where he teaches Communicative English for academic purposes.

PREFACE

Vandita Dharni is a writer who wields her pen with great panache. Divided into three sections, her book, An Alchemy of Musings, is indeed a delight for every poetry lover. The first part comprises 68 poems- pure and pristine in their composition and content. These poems have the power to delve deep into sensitive souls and keep burrowing till they have made snug places for themselves with their multi-layered, metaphorical, and intertextual grandeur. I will call her a cerebral poet, whose heart throbs and pulsates with palpable tenderness.

In the first section, one of the poems that I really liked, was The Mist, not merely because of her beautiful depiction of nature, but because of its many nuances, the last lines sent me into a brown study.

"This must be the last halt I tell myself- Am I the sojourner here?
Let's do something quirky, a freefall
Then will the mist cover me too?"

Through the immensely impactful poem, 'My Own Story', she seems to be telling the story of each one of us in these pernicious times.

"Teaching sans eyes and ears has become habitual
I teach in my sleep, ranting philosophies
of Plato, Aristotle and others I forget now.
Immersed in an ocean of thought,
my head reels with numbers, names and theories
. . . .
"Out, out brief candle!" echoes aloud in my ears.
Am I hallucinating or insane?

Showers of love is very poignantly penned, and the solitude and longing of the woman in the poem wrenches the heart.

"No visitor called today, not even blackbirds
Only the rusty creak of the door, unlatched
and the piercing draughts crept in,
flexing their way to keep her company.

She holds a raindrop in her palm
to savour his fragrance still warm
Old melodies wing in her heart
of initials untraced on her spangled wrist."

A Tribute to the Ganges is a poem, where I believe, she has outdone herself.

Her personification of the Ganges, the innovative similes and metaphors that she has so meticulously used, have a certain finesse, and a long-lasting appeal.

"Today, I ink you into parchment skin
Combing back those raven tresses
dishevelled but not fossilized by time or distance
into postcard memories.
Rajnigandha kisses mist my glass panes,
Yet, my children's paper boats I pray
will flow you back someday."

Vandita Dharni has a powerful vocabulary, and impressive diction which leaves an indelible impression on the mind and heart – 'a phlegmatic silence on puckered lips', 'cuckoo's hush', 'summer's searing tongue', 'unrelenting paperweights of unrest', are some words which you want to keep savouring, over and over again.

The second section is a collection of Roseate Sonnets- an experimental form of sonnet created by the versatile and erudite scholar, Dr. Ampat Koshy, inspired by the symbol of the rose. Its fourteen lines comprise two quatrains, followed by a couplet, and then the last quatrain, in which the first line starts with R, the next with an O, the third with S, and the last with an E, thus forming the acrostic ROSE. All the sonnets have been penned equally wonderfully, but the majestic beauty of the acrostic in the sonnet, Eau de Vie Nights (A tribute to Chopin] is something that makes it rise above the rest of the sonnets.

"Rise up now, conjure your feisty accented mazurka,
Obliquely interspersing diatonic pitches with chromatic scales
Stay a while, it's still night, the menacing battle isn't lost yet
Ever so alive- I feel your pulse in my blue veins, I'm in love again."

Like the Enigma in her poem of the same name, Vandita Dharni has done a remarkable job of unfurling her golden magnificence in her spectacularly penned, multi-nuanced poems.
Her prose -poems are marked by a tender elegance and beautiful imagery, the words pirouetting on the page, making you sway with their lyrical cadence.
Indeed, her versatile pen paints vivid pictures, each hue offering the reader something to mull over, something to nestle close to. Without any fear of sounding hyperbolic, let me mention that this book is indeed a work of art, and a joy to be forever cherished.

May her verses continue to serenade the world for years to come, with their poetic grace.
Dr. Santosh Bakaya

Winner of Reuel International Award [2014] for Oh Hark! , Setu Award for excellence [2018] for her 'stellar contribution to world literature, [Setu, bilingual Journal Pittsburgh, USA], the First Keshav Malik Award [2019] for her 'entire staggeringly prolific and quality conscious oeuvre', essayist, poet, novelist, editor, TEDx Speaker, Dr. Santosh Bakaya has been acclaimed for her poetic biography of Bapu, Ballad of Bapu [Vitasta, Delhi, 2015].
 Her other books are:
Only in Darkness can you see the Stars [A Biography of Martin Luther King Jr. Vitasta, 2019] Songs of Belligerence [Authors Press, 2020]
Morning Meanderings, [e-book Blue Pencil, 2020]
Her other two collaborative e-books: Vodka by the Volga [with Dr. Koshy, Blue Pencil, 2020]
From Prinsep Ghat to Peer Panjal[with Gopal Lahiri, Blue Pencil, 2021] have been Amazon bestsellers.
Runcible Spoons and Pea-green Boats is her latest book [Poetry, Authors press, 2021,

ACKNOWLEDGEMENTS

The journey of a lifetime has on board many an experience that sprouts many an inspiration, The diversity from these sources that contribute in this splendid sojourn makes it worth the while in my poetic aspirations. Emotions do become an intrinsic part which coagulate into sensual and modernist poetic musings. The conception of this book occurred while writing for the Napowrimo on the Significant League, a popular group on Facebook.

First and foremost, Prashant Gupta and the Great Indian Book Tour can take a bow for creating a beautiful home for my book by publishing and promoting it through diverse platforms.

Timothy Payton, thank you my dear friend for giving 'An Alchemy of Musings' its identity. Your aesthetic portrayal that brushes the cover and face of this book has added the vibrance and radiance, not to forget your magnanimity displayed through your paintings for one of my earlier books, 'Rippling Overtures.'

Dr. Ampat Varghese Koshy a sincere appreciation for the glowing introduction and Dr. Santosh Bakaya a heartfelt acknowledgement for an outstanding preface that have added value to my humble offering. As mentors and a guiding source, it was indeed fortunate to have the privilege of working together as co-authors and editors of an anthology titled, 'Ruddy Ravens, Cheshire Cats and Rusty Rats' which was a roaring success, having spiralled to the sixth position on the Amazon's list of bestsellers.

Brenda Mohammed the author of forty-five books and founder admin of How to Write for Success Literary Forum and Florabelle Lutchman my very dear friends for sparing their valuable time to share their thoughts on my book in the blurb.

My family who has been my mainstay, a source of constant and consistent support and love who never let me lose sight of my goal. They were my best friends and my greatest critics without whom the book would never have reached its final lap.

Last but not least, those whom I may have forgotten to mention but nevertheless left an indelible impression on my book and life. Thankyou from the bottom of my heart!

Vandita Dharni

A BALLET OF LIFE
(Inspired by 'The Nutcracker' movie)

Last night my room turned into a battlefield
Of mice, tin soldiers and dolls
The room grew by itself, no care for norms.
Then in the mirror, I saw a fairy or was she a queen
holding the key to my fate?
Some say she is the virtuoso who holds dominion
of the Land of Sweets where fountains bleed of them.
Her feathery fuchsia strands stitched themselves into
the hemmed bodice of her tainted glory
which made me recall the words someone said,
"There's more value in evil than brocade."

Her sinister designs were concealed in folds of a tutu
while she slunk into shoes, yanking them in a rond de jambe
curling herself into Tchaikovsky's celesta, she performed
an etendre ses jambes, turning people to toys in a plan to
destroy the world,
No music box could play her tune backwards
Nor could she animate good for evil.
She glissers on the floor with her pointe shoes, pirouetting
on veins that throbbed with life/ death.
She is the shadow, dark and fleeting-
An angel of death, her eyes hold an evil gaze.
"There's no value in evil than brocade," I say,
as she gradually pierces the shards and returns
to the porcelain she once was- a doll, a mere invention,
Nothing more.

A FAMILIAR TAP

To melt your turquoise heart and in anorexic fits of hysteria
I want to become a sliver of your radiance, burying what
craves to be unleashed. Crimson surges coursing in my
veins,
Peacock waves warble thoughtlessly morphing into lips,
running over me like carbuncles clinging on to the conch,
trapping swishing melodies.

Each balmy tomorrow springs a whiff of you in scented
earthy glades where I saunter sometimes in hope of finding
your breath nestled in leaves bleached in your sweat –
lukewarm with a tinge of salt. As I shake the knobbly
boughs, a dewdrop trickles down my thigh. Ah! The scent of
you drenches me and I bloom into a blue primrose.

Deeper and deeper, I explore the vacuum that fills me from
within- you, treading upon cold vestibules where the air
has a hostile crispness like crunchy peanut buttered toasts
with a hint of morning cappuccino lining the cup we shared
together, still do.

Tonight, it's another cold misty night and I sense the same
yearning ricocheting the walls of my mind, corroding the
epithelial tissue with overtures defying gravity. A familiar
tap and a rush of adrenaline enveloping the solitary confines
of
a thalassophile.

CAUGHT BETWEEN HEMISPHERES

Eyelids nestle silver crescents
of my wakeful morrows,
Sleep pulls me into a latitude of night.
I tug at its covert embrace, interposed
with the dynamics of shifting hemispheres
harnessing the punctum of compromise.

The silver crusted night
hangs its hemispheres around my neck
-dew drops in concentric rings,
I scatter them on my feet as ghungroos,
sailing on a silver browed arc
threading love ghazals in the dark.

Their melody resonates, churning my musings
in a glass of homemade ginger wine,
The crescents on their onward journey move
with an aromatic rush of adrenaline.
between hemispheres of sleep and waking
waiting for dawn to melt them away.

(First Published in the Fasihi Magazine, July 2020)

IN THE HEART OF THE FOREST

Ripples of water swirl into dolphins
serrated jaws gulp them, in vortices
of a night's death. Profound as secrets
on the grass tapestry you observe the
fishermen heaving, flexing those nylons.
Eyes glued, nets floating for a wedge
without compunction to surface out of the
deep and present itself, the prey
born out of vastness, your imagination
as all born into existence do, dribbling in
incarceration. Then the sudden swerve,
the adrenaline, the agile writhing
of a body at the surface as it veers. And what
ensues is the backflow, a wriggling, swiveling
of a tail fin

Withdrawing. What did I
envision before I made my way here-
A ripped leaf, a windmill
Or my own brokenness splintered into-
Tongues, licking the alchemy of each fear
spawning into a multitude of helices
sluggishly finning on a fulcrum of fallacies,
Diving into the current, until you trapped
each fish and hooked them into an obelisk.

He decants the splinters back into the
jaws of the ocean – not a salmon, not a fish

Nothing that bore the buoyancy of life-
just a flapping oar, a rush of blood. Then,
surfaces your own reflection- dark and
Cold like death. As dusk gathers, lingers-
the tremulous water buries in glazed
skin. Stilted rays fall in simmering, crimson
needles on the ocean.

Between the seams of open sky,
clouds spread their wings
cradling tangerine threads with a coldness,
swallowing up the dusk,
your father's silhouette, the ocean
thc fish, that flapping oar.

And .....
a tireless writhing continues-
Call it imagination, a journey beyond,
An engulfing of words tethered in
a fortress of night, deepening its fate lines
on the sprawling archipelago of North Sentinel
in the Andaman and Nicobar islands,
It bursts open at the seams again, splattering blood
in the heart of the forest. Somewhere close
the Sentinelese have speared an American national.

CATAMARAN DREAMS

On sails my fuschia catamaran
into the ritournelle of my song
Sipping, swirling, satiating
Dressing and undressing passion
in my floral sarong.
I surrender to its melody so tender
wishing night would never surrender
to a diaphanous morn.
The firmament yanks its sails
to rain confetti on moss covered pathways
Ravished in their numbness, I gape
 and drape them around frozen contours:

snug in the comfort of their velvety wings
flying through enchanting vistas in my head
In this orgiastic frenzy, lies my vulnerability
entangled in thickets of blackberries.
I catch them susurrating,
threading love notes
in my sarong streaked with damp night.

(First Published in the Fasihi Magazine, July 2020)

AN ENIGMA

On autumn nights she passes me by
in aurelius dreams, her eyes dazzle mine,
The hangover lasts until I awaken
from the realm of a gilded horizon
that stings my skin with nectarine.
Is she the yellow narcissus
fluttering in my heart
or the incandescent flame that glows
in my eyes on candle lit nights?

My heart melts in the sorbet twilight
floating on sussurous wings
Chartering lands, skies with cotton brows
copper rooftops- this utopia full blown.
Call it an enigma or the hush of a bewitching zephyr,
there is no escaping her intoxicating spell.

Entranced by her ephemerality I succumb
as she unfurls her golden magnificence
upon my searing breast.

She is the golden firefly.

(First Published in the Fasihi Magazine, July 2020)

APHRODITE

The azure swirls its charm,
melting misty flakes into heaven's tears
scattering and pattering a mellifluous refrain
like the first kiss of summer rain.
She bathes in an aphrodisiac sensuality
her bosom heaving like forget-me-nots;
Close, a sparrow trills in the woodland green
echoing her presence in the glade.

Is she for real or dregs of a sinfionetta?
Her lips curl into crimson petals
while carmine leaves capture the enigma
of her haunting fragrance,
enveloping her in a sublunary ambience.
She pirouettes each night
to the music of the spheres
while the song pregnant in her womb
taps in her veins like sap dripping -
drip, drop, drippity drip
from a tree that once sprouted love's roots.

On star dust nights she is the moon
with her jasmine tresses, igniting a heart that
passionately throbs for her.
On others, she is the myrtle in full bloom
Savouring the ambrosial air,
until she turns into an exquisite bird
dissolving into a lingering swan song.

LIFE GIVES US A SECOND CHANCE

A dissipated life flickers into a candle
till all the wax melts to mingle with mire.

Transgressions are clothes that don't fit, faded, frayed
worn to hide the naked truth, a price we pay.

Yet, they only conceal apprehensions
singeing our skin, peeling our delusions.

Let's crawl back on the ribbon
for at the end of darkness, is a glimmer

that will dry the dregs of guilt away
when these clothes are hung out.

Life has a purpose so don't give up yet
the candle may burn out, not the wick set.

No matter how deep one may have sunk
there is hope and always a second chance.

CROSSROADS OF LIFE

On the asphalt
of our life sometimes
faults sink
in regrets stink
and we seek
possibilities
solutions to overcome…
Then in darkness, despair is birthed
and we think
it's over
it's lost forever,
hopeless
dead…
yet
think again…
mistakes make us human,
vulnerable,
fragile,
faith rekindles dying embers
to feed a brighter tomorrow…
so live.

SHARDS OF LOVE

On that bridge lie shards
piercing feet of captivity deep,
etching scars upon my heart
when I tread upon cobblestones.
Dust licks off blood that splatters
in eyeballs of the sun
but the splinters remain embedded in feet,
They impale grouchily
flickering as fading beams
within a waxen chambered heart.

Drumbeats of a woodpecker
pecking at my heart,
drills out verses that nestle there.
I yank the woodpecker from my dream
What does he want now? My heart is his,
Battered and scattered
across the verdant valley that blossoms love.
Mystical murmurs of the rivulet
carry a melody yonder to the azure
wrapping a heart bandaged, stitched
in a motley coat of carnations,
I reclaim it after all these years
Yet it still breathes,
severed in two.

(First Published in the Fasihi Magazine, July 2020)

REIGNITED HOPES

When night slips into the moon's chalice
the sky is set ablaze in its resplendence,
Orbs glimmer through lovers' eyes
sprouting buds of the passion flower
on feathery stems to energize
a lingering kiss of aromatic liquorice.

Manic dreams are all cattywampus
Rekindling fantasies in chaotic minds floating
downstream like goldfish swimming about
on a cul de sac of muddled seaweed-
a crystal world inexorably enclosing.
They cling on, hopeful that a nirvana
will release them from its clutches.

Smoldering flames crackle up the hearth,
hissing secrets only walls have heard
consuming them bit by bit
until they are swallowed in an inferno's belly
wall skins sucked by an apricot glaze.

Crimson lips still hold a lustrous glow
thawing pinnacles covered with snow,
Entangled branches sway to the moaning wind
swirling dew drops in caskets of foliage
Those concentric rings reignite fire in hearts
stringing amber beads before autumn departs.

(First Published in the Fire Anthology, 2020)

THE CLAIRVOYANT'S CIGAR

In forbidding circles
night treads on smoky clouds,
convulsively flickering in a candle's flame.
Hollow voices ricochet near fjords
Life's sojourn aching to a close
in Cannabis moments vapourized.

Lost in the crepuscule haze of solitude,
a broken winged butterfly
flutters its paper wings-
life's breath, one deceitful breath
enshrouded by the hostile mist- dark
on a suffocatingly treacherous night.

"Hussshhhhhh!"
the clairvoyant vapes
predicting the highs and lows,
now sunk in the residue of waxen stubs-
false promises he spouts to himself,
snuffed out by his voodoo chants-
"Husshhh!" I see frail fingers resting,
replicating burnt out cigar ends
imprinting crimson on jaded greenbacks.

A night drunk in marijuana haze
Life swims full circle. "Hush!"

(First Published in SETU magazine. Feb, 2021)

THE HAVEN I YEARN FOR

While wrinkled mountains beckon, I follow
promptings of a heart gossamered in illusions,
The azure envelops the hamlets that pass me by.
Beneath, the valley spruces up with
rhododendrons, wild Primula and purple violets.
Their virginal appeal so raw, unexplored and surreal
and I ask myself, is this paradise on earth for real?

The placid lake allures me to a panorama
where secrets unfold, new and old,
Others wrapped like sweetmeats in wrappers gold
whisper sonatas thawing the iceberg within.
Hush! All norms I abandon so not to regret,
I explore its magical beauty scouring vistas
before my throbbing grows into a sunset.

Into a geisha I turn- a hypnotic sway of hips,
immersing into a jazz of rapturous bliss,
The flower bedecked sail boats
rim my eyes- gliding on the lake
until they disappear in the wilderness.
The blue peafowl preens its crest
dipping into the dew kissed petals of dawn.

My wings transport me to beauteous terrains
where fresh water springs blow pan pipes,
transforming thorns into emerald diadems.
A landscape that man's cruel hand has not yet scarred
with his rapacity to gormandize.
A land Kalpa Kinnaur, where time stands still
I savour it knowing, I shall never have my fill.

UTOPIA

Often nature springs surprises on a canvas
I splash it with hues of my heart
Bluish tints for ridges, kohl lashes for clouds
and a lush green valley unfolding dawn's first sigh.

Yellow Narcissi and rhododendrons blush pink
to explode the valley with a riot of colour,
intoxicating like jasmine, a panacea for nerves
as I pause for breath in rapt amazement.

The vertiginous views are breathtaking,
Yet the yearning rises in the pit of your stomach
and the heady smell of luscious peaches and apricots
pull me into their fantasy world.

A land where dreams sit in tinkling troikas
as starry lanterns glimmer their sensuousness,
Squirrels nibble on pinecones, rubbing their noses
 scurrying across desolate woods till summer beckons.

The boughs stretch their fingers along sluggish streams
ruffling them like a moth's papery wings,
'Tis another season now, decked in ochre and vermillion hues
'Sleep golden summer until autumn her conch will blow.'

Coral mornings breathe in the mist of tranquility
Sentinel mountains peer with pride standing majestically.
Myriad birds echo the moaning wind's refrain,
"Oh, hark!" they cheep as frosty winter crawls again.

WAXEN MUSINGS

In a thicket of silence, it sprouts
sometimes like mint flavouring your tea,
groping the handle of your sublunary door
till you unlock it into eternity.
Gravity overhangs herringbone cobwebs
suspended in a muddled-up brain.
Knotting threads on the penumbrae
of a dishevelled sunset,
The racy tongue swirls mouthfuls
of filtered sunshine- choking, splattering seeds,
erupting from craters of twilight.
In an ellipsis, I resonate the cacophony
of multiple words jarring, ruminating on
black feathery lids of sleep and waking;
tossing them into reflective inflections
silent, breathing, unmoved
in the sterility of the soul
flowing into cascades
of molten viscosity dripping onto
an envelope, sealing it with promises-
now waxen musings.

WHIMSICAL INK

Whimsical ink seamlessly splatters on parallel lines
to find purpose, pirouetting on mind's clay,
Its wings carry alphabets to distant climes
forming swirls in blue Curacao with a dash of lime.

Oftentimes on this sea, thoughts are released
cradled in ships, scouring oceans to sail
they toss the moon above a creak with ease
and share a thousand letters, frisking slender tails.

Commas and flat button caesuras greet words as they pause
while an errant clause ends with a dazed exclamation mark,
Others live a constrained parenthesis existence due to a flaw
and then embarking on a sojourn, lose their spark.

I try to erase obtrusive and garbled words
Yet they stare nonchalantly, through hooded eyes
brandishing rapiers to dodge me, on the run
their hideous presence more pronounced with no compromise.

As I flick endless pages of my mind
Bleeding words accost me with fake smiles
that died long ago, manacled in fetters unkind
on frayed ochre pages of classified files.

Seasons purloin the essence of these symbols
hurling them on stony pages of the heart,
where they splatter ink on walls of indifference
with no emotions left to brood, they depart.

They hobble on dust paved tracks
Melting clouds of insularity and scorn,
pattering on window panes turning their backs
documenting histories for seeds unborn.

THE LOST SONNET

Survive I shan't in shadows of your curse
so be condemned for stealing my verse,
My sonnets ne'er shall dwell within stony walls you bred-
a reflection of truth are they, not a birdsong that breaks its
thread.
Collect now I their fragments, torn, worn on my face as scars,
Two eyes gleamed, then scattered them yonder towards the
stars.
Desperate was I, awaiting the clouds to rain them down as
tears,
What's blustered them back is the zephyr after all those years,
back to the withered Elm that grew cold in your vicinity.
And as you lay cold, I let them slip into your coffin without
toxicity
for I am told they keep no secrets, the dead never lie.
Your tongue will now unwillingly, breathe them undefiled,
eternity will etch them into an epitaph on your grave
such virtue flows through their veins, the veins I gave.

MY PARADISE

Our heritage home was a haven
with fuschia and rufous painted on its skin,
where walls grew a million stories
masked by murals and traditional paintings.
The furniture a polished elegant mahogany,
sunk its cabriole legs into the winsome luxuriance
of a carpet that would transform into a den of grandma's tales.
The floor gleamed ivory especially on nights streaked
by careless paws, frequenting nooks and corners friskily.
The crystal chandelier lit up a million eyes,
stirring up young and old to belt out old numbers
to the strains of a Spanish guitar.
Tables donned blue and white porcelain
with an air of vintage sophistication,
Yet ensconced in the fireplace,
the warmth of a mother's heart lay.
Glasses clinked with cheery home-brewed ginger ale
and guffaws and Elvis Presley and dollops of nostalgia.

The French windows mullioned in white
my gateway to paradise, stood tall
wearing velvet drapes to restrict summer's eyes.
From here I'd watch mynahs and koels
holding conference, perching on silver oak branches,
My beady eyes would follow parakeets dusting their wings
flirting with the wanton wind, kissing their plumes.
A contingent of ants often surveyed drams
nibbling bread crumbs with gusto

strewn on blades of satin grass.
At a distance, a scarecrow balanced his pot head
on a tree as fearless rodents invaded his home.
Tangerine, grapefruit and guava trees
grew exotic roots deep into our hearts
suckling thirsty mouths, splattering elixir
onto scruffy, mischievous hands.
These memories still warm my heart
a treasure I'll nestle forever
even in the umbrage of the guava groves.

SWEET POISON
(In memory of Sylvia Path)

So anguished was her frame
trapped in a labyrinthine hourglass,
She lived in splinters of despair
incarcerated in the epiphany of time
her miniscule frame cracked within.
Seeking release from earthly woes
she spawned innumerable sonnets,
But envy disguised in a slithering snake
suckled on her snowy white breast,
starved for a mortal sacrifice.
They gouged out her intestines,
hoping she would weep and wail
but all she left was a trail,
a trail not of blood
but one of a life plucked untimely.
Not measured in yards of infamy
or steeped in vainglory
but smouldering, surrendering to none
but her own self.
Glaring at her audacity, they loathed her
They were menacing as Medusa's gaze.
Yet, she was a sandcastle, illusory, fragile.
Her frail fingers penned a dying note,
her epitaph- wrought with labour and grief:

> *'A Dissipated life*
> *that evoked tales and elegies*

on capricious lovers and concubines
now fades with the setting sun.'

Fade? Never will she
Not until those shards piercing her heart
splutter her sacrosanct name.

She has the last laugh
scoffing nonchalantly.

THE WEEDS
(In Memory of Edgar Allen Poe 1809-1849)

Into corners, I bury weeds- entangled
in what lies within and without
in the sifting and incipient drifting-
the debris of a withered life,
Compressed in pages of poesy
dog earing a past, blighted
bursting open-into a montage of images
desecrating the lattice of his overgrown solace.

Here, rests the shovel
snipping Spear thistles unwarranted,
those that germinated into cycles of deceit
glowering at their rival's defeat.
The fire of Prometheus seething in Rufus' eyes
blinking through dank tunnels
where Oizys held sway.
Strife slithering through insalubrious pockets,
drenched in sweat and alcohol
a containment zone of mortified fears.

Whose life I contemplate?
I glance at the pauper's grave-
My nascent tears nestle there
and in those dog-eared pages demystified
I see myself, a part of me dead.

Then and now, the time he lived
I thrust the obituary ruthlessly bold
thriving on Rufus' weeds of acrimony
as Edgar's blue veins run ice cold.

(First Published in SETU Magazine Feb, 2020)

THE MANGLED WOMB

Her hair cascaded down her sun kissed skin
fluttering on the dewy breath of morning,
Those withered veins hung silken beads
on skeletal boughs that once held her silence.

Blow your forked murmurs you light winged dryad
blow them to another land where sunsets never return,
Find me those visceral remnants
of a woman who let her unborn dreams burn.

In vestry arches and stained-glass windows,
Remains of another day rest, whispering a benediction in vain.
Tangled in a heap of bones she grapples
at the grave, her petalled eyes moistening again.

No fire can ignite his compassion
For his heart is a marbled tomb,
No glade nor sun can augur respite
to her mangled, violated womb.

Crows squawk at the setting sun
searing through the cumulous,
Every moan silenced in his thunder
seeks answers for his blunder.

Deep in the shadow of night she breaks-
the silence that once made her heart quake.

SOLITUDE

Night you hold my breath in
wisps of solitude,
Leaves of a dank past
flutter on tree boughs
An impassioned cold haze
drips its residue in a mortified gaze.

Poppies of his crimson wreath
wrap me in the unkempt heath.
Traces of magnolia still lie on the sill
where he left them cold and withered
in a heartache, A pregnant cloud
yanked them into wispy, white butterflies
fluttering into sleepy strands of day.

Fog creeps through/in
wildly soaking, his breath
now a gasp, a flutter
And whoosh- ---------- [silence]

The trappings of a night
tug at my heart, pulling over
A nightcap of tears.

CHILDHOOD DECONSTRUCTED

Claps of thunder in the leaden sky
echo the earth's death knell,
Decayed stumps thirst for rain
in the womb of night.

Musings orbit an ellipsis of thoughts
A rented catacomb is my mind
where they glimmer, birthing moons
 that wane into dank, gnarled ribs.

Luscious cherry blossoms hung overhead
draped with blessings of a birdsong
Yonder, the gush and rustle
throbbed in the arteries of another winter
cold, saturnine, pregnant with coagulated emotions.

This was my childhood deconstructed
As tiny palms and pigtails waved
swallowing the dust of memories.

A EUNOIA

I am not given to rhetoric
nor do I constrain wisdom

in bottlenecked ideologies.
Their cinnamon skin wears out

bleeding latex down to the bone
Unfeeling, in their orgiastic fusion,

hissing in my ears
muted replicas of green serpents.

I hear their thrum echoing
in a deafening drone.

Blue veined denizens in a logical fallacy
unleash their mammoth fury,

Growing resistant to gravity,
wind displacing their pollen

Until they find acceptance -

A eunoia.

HOW TO MAKE

The usual day is strung with possibilities
on boughs of my mindscape,

the thirsty tongue spurts its juice
impertinently chewing on nutty seeds.

Those possibilities I pluck one by one.
Some soured/salty by summer's sweat,

Some warmed by a honeyed morn's kiss
Throwing inhibition to the wind.

The girl in me blushes an apple
Letting adrenaline rush to take over.

Nor will their interim gloom fade
Nor ripened years spent in the glade.

I crush their pulp to make a vinaigrette
A bit of cyanide couldn't harm

For time's blender squashes them
into a pulpy yeast of uncertainty.

Thus, brewing in its sugars, flavours fuse
into an organic delusion of night-

alcohol fermenting into ethanoic acid
the metamorphosis now near complete.

I pour that into a bottle labelled – A C Vinegar
My antioxidant for the day.

DISINHERITANCE

Yet somewhere, my heart misses a beat
I smell drones, stone cold,
I rub their memory off my palms
But the hum continues
snaking through my heart-
a refugee in both climes.

All is lost- my parents too, we all are
lost in the vortex of disinheritance
and I am caught between longitudinal time zones
waiting for dawn to melt the yearning away.

I cross the rubicon, wrestling with anxiety
As the journey continues,
my moksha and nirvana
seep into blue veins of my new country
where I die every day
to be reborn again.

A LANGUAGE UNKNOWN

Flowers speak a language unknown,
echoing tales of unrequited love
a glow with virginal rays from heaven above.
The Morning Glory adorns herself in azure and pearls,
Her waxen wings glisten, breathing hope on a sultry day
dropping kisses on dewy beds of green
and spraying silken hues on parched landscapes.
She unfurls her serpentine tendrils,
her succulent lips quivering,
kissing the carpeted green with her vines,
drenching them in a fragrance divine.

Migratory hummingbirds nestle on her warm breasts
warbling and roosting in marbled crests.
They wallow, humming the melody of Spring,
Somewhere in the woodland, they saunter up a trestle
to steal the symphony of cascading waterfalls, whispering
to winds along forlorn pathways. Often, they echo a melody
drowning winter's fog and infusing mirth to a world bereft.

Contrary to this, is another flaming beauty- the Narcissi.
Harbingers of spring they bob their cheery heads tall
pirouetting in porcelain pinafores, flaunting yellow satin.
Sealing frosty winter with a thawing kiss,
They herald Spring's euphoria with a heady floral fragrance
alluring many a lonesome pilgrim.
They conjure up the legend of Narcissus,

an architect of his own doom. Their lustre enchants
fair Persepone too entrapped in perpetual Hades' gloom.
Bees and butterflies flit around this legacy,
A carousel of perfume wafting through the air.
Endearingly, they breathe hope and renewal
Unblemished yet oblivious to fate,
buzzing a language unknown.
Both of them unique yet they echo
the same language, the language of love.

SILENCE

Her amber eyes reflected a fury,
the lighthouse on an ocean.
Her restive heart fluttered-
a tornado of endless dreams, gypped
by the ferocity of an ill- timed winter
harshly extinguishing a burnt- out candle.

The spectral night slithered through
her serpentine neck, splattering
rubies across her warm belly-
Her crimson lips smiled nonchalantly
while the magma erupted within her.

The staccato ticking of a clock silenced
those lifeless hands in a dirge,
A whirring fan emboldened just above
diffused incensed hymns, dispelling winter's curse.

Dulcet necklaces hung in the air -
Hollow tubes entangled in a labyrinth of memories
Ah! The smell of dankness embossed
in her marble lips now waxen cold.

Quivering veins ingested with Nembutal
sedated her nonchalance into a stupor
seeping into the quietus of night.

The azure sky smeared the kohl of her eyes
into the canvas of night,
leaving skeletal trees to behold an oppressive silence.
The wind howled through the feathered mist
filigreed with fresh carnation wreaths
drenched in the fragrance of night.
The thorn from her lily- white breast yanked out
had lingered still like gangrene-
The deathly dance grew untamed
until the chaff blew away into the wind.

A star twinkles in the dead of night
And the billowing wind moans-

Euthanasia.

(First Published in RIC Journal in Nov 2020)

POETRY MISUNDERSTOOD

"*Poetry is the spontaneous overflow of powerful feelings*"
so aptly propagated and digested too,
Until very recently, young Hudibras tumbled upon my head.
In an aching moment of revulsion, shriven
I nosedived, grabbing him like manna from heaven
scanning him circumspectly, lock stock and barrel
owing to his chivalrous exploits and with an intent to gorman-
dize.
But to my disappointment, it was a useless exercise.
I decided I'd quaff the remnants of my coffee
that smirked at me from a cylindrical mug in utmost glee,
Reminding me of profounder thoughts
how Prufrock measured his life in coffee spoons.
More often than not, on certain occasions I do get invited to
high teas
but one that enthralled me with crochet and lace
was the famous tea at the Hampton Court palace
In all respects, a visitor's paradise
until I heard one night the Baron sliced off a lock
that exasperated poor Belinda to run amok.
Methinks, I searched for respite in Wordsworth.
So perchance at another tea of lesser worth,
I vehemently articulated a point to my father
"Child is the father of Man," spluttered I rhetorically
But before I knew, a punch settled on my aquiline nose.
Adding to my misery, mother quoted Prelutsky, (I froze)
"Be glad your nose is on your face." (Sigh!)
That concluded all discussions and deliberations henceforth.

My defunct brain took shrine in Kipling
I consoled myself convulsively blabbering,
"East is East, and West is West, and never the twain shall meet,"
I explored many a book, scrutinized them cover to cover
transforming father's library into my self- created den
Where Milton advised me that it was better to
"Reign in hell than serve in heaven."
Which heaven?
A heaven that created absurd days and nights
Where fishes flew and forests walked on earth
for a donkey to be birthed?
"How ludicrous!" I contemplated.
My discerning eye keenly surveyed books
Giving me the most menacing looks
Perturbed was I, but one lured me in due course
So, I mustered the courage to take recourse
Its dog ears glared at me aghast, it was Rene Viviene
writing about strange hair and how she saw
"as one sees a flower fade-
On your mouth, like summer auroras,
The withered smile of an old whore."
A whore, an analogy? In sooth, I grimaced
and for another book I paced.
I had often heard it said, "A thing of beauty is a joy forever"
But for me it was a question of now or never.
So, I immersed myself in the Metaphysicals like Donne and
Marvell
My weary eyes could not fathom
How could a compass be compared to lovers?
I mean didn't it have piercing ends

Or did lovers grow them too or maybe three?
In a dilemma was I when mother reprimanded me
noticing my room, a vicious mess
I had to straighten it all under duress.
Captivated by the thought, I began to settle and unsettle
not realizing I looked a spectacle.
Talking of spectacles, my mind wandered
drunk deeply in thoughts of my bespectacled grandmother
a voracious reader with a keen eye for poetry,
several books she had gifted me secretly.
But Macavity always intrigued my playful senses
a cat with magical powers to plunder and disappear,
missing from the scene of crime as he was certainly "not there."
My restless hand began to rummage and dig
before supper I pilfered time for Dahl's obnoxious pig
who could solve sums in his brain
a brain of sorts, I winced, frowning, "What a pain!"
But when I frowned, I remembered Browning
an optimist who always left me frowning.
The only poem that really regaled me
hovered around the flippant monk, Fra Lippo Lippi
always caught red handed "at an alley's end
where sportive ladies left "their doors ajar."
Doors why not hearts, I failed to decipher?
Monks were not the only recipients of jest
Bishops and popes too were disrobed at the reader's behest
Carroll mistook a pope for a bar of mottled soap.
Who invented mottled soap anyway, is my query?
I'm certain it must have existed before young Lochinvar
the dauntless knight who slipped on it

in a feverish fit to woo his future bride
thus leaving this poor bridegroom helplessly,
"dangling his bonnet and plume."
Finally, quod erat demonstrandum,
fee fee fo I fum,
It is best to mend the hearts I have broken
by now I have lost count, of so many have I spoken
The Bible teaches us to love our neighbours
Frost reiterates, 'Good fences make good neighbors.'
But he also asserts, "Why do they make good neighbors? Isn't it
Where there are cows? But here there are no cows."
So, I rest my case but not my cause. Or was it cows?

A FURRY ENCOUNTER
(Two dogs- one a loafer, the other a pedant)

The searing golden orb cuts across crossroads
where two contrasting dogs, strikingly familiar make an entry.
The first - a regular loafer on the spin, exploring an ant horde
and the other, a foxy faced spitz, glossed with pedantry.

"Woof, woof why're you strutting on my territory,
don't you know that attributes to trespassing?
I scramble up walls, brambles and thickets in a flurry
navigating through filth that you'd rather not scurry."

"Oft have I noticed your calloused paws scrunch around
Isn't that a dry bone peeping through your canines?
I bet you unearthed it from garbage where you were found
rummaging and resurrecting putrid waste from bins."

"Hey, woof, woof I live by impulses and instincts
flicking swarms of flies with my rough, bare paws,
I frisk about entertaining damsels with my antics
they bark, whisking their tails, oblivious to my flaws."

"Sigh! Your unkempt nails and repulsive yellowed canines
the whiffs you emit without a doubt augur your notoriety,
Your coat is scruffier than a coal hole so unrefined
and don't you dare transfer those repulsive creepy crawlies."

"The cockiness in your tone is way too insulting
My instincts tell me you're just a finicky ole' chap
who yaps and yaps until no one's a-listening
not brushing or manicuring, all you need is a rap."

"I'm certain the outdoors is where you must be
playing hop scotch with hoi polloi, devoid of class.
Exclusivity certainly doesn't gel with mediocrity
your breath is malodorous and taste is crass."

"Every tree in this park I sprinkle and mark everyday
My muzzle snoops into corners that you can never guess.
Cuckoos and crickets chirp seeing me so gay
and never frown though I'm always undressed."

"My heavily plumed tail can swipe away all my flaws
roller relaxers massage and rub a dub all day my tired nerves
The succulent flesh I relish will tempt your ravenous maws
Pshaw! My outer coat hides all my extra curves."

"Stop niggling, high headed brat, you're pretentious and silly
Keep your sophistication tucked inside your velvety bed
the trainer with your leash is beckoning willy nilly,
while I'm a merry vagabond, with the azure over my head."

FEUILLE MORTE

The season of yearning, transition
loss, carpeted by russet ashes of a departed summer.
Cloven leaves, chestnut trees,
Crunched in a timeless ode- Autumn.

Nothing frames my window but hieroglyphics
in carmine and crimson tufts of the meadow,
Red-breasted robins flap about their rusty tunics
whirling burnished copper clouds across the azure.

Evenings ripen in the zest of apple picking
conspiring with a honeyed relish of harvest time,
Another rutting season culls as many a buck is preyed
and dreamcatchers sway to lull a sparrow's trill.

The Helenium flutters its red velvet wings, waiting
for the wolf moon to ride the river's watery tusks
Far in the valley between the hills, lambs bleat
as the air winnows a woody aromatic musk.

RESIDUE OF MEMORIES

Frayed sepia photographs curl into my palms
calloused now with vagaries of time,
Old manuscripts conjure moments
lived and relived in rusty suitcases,
of visages archived in mothballs-
a familiar scrawl on a pad, traditional artifacts
collected on a trip up North, old coins, trinkets and rain.

It was a utopic getaway from the whirring buzz
where we could smell pines and Lindon blossoms
as dawn blanched to velvet dusk
Turacos, bearded vultures and rock partridges
flapping across the palm dotted valleys
and the landscape travelled in our lenses
as we soaked aromas of mimosa and fig trees.

My eyelids now heavy turn into sleep chambers-
'Bring in those rose scented candles, will you?
The ones that spin a farrago of fantasy and reality
Put them by the mantle shelf, the fireplace is warm
And the woollen shawl is still wrapped around me
the one you bought me with your first salary.
Yes, and I still haven't forgotten the rain.'

EIGHT O' CLOCK

I ignore the alarm buzzing in
the pell-mell of my morning fuzz
I run down the block, stocking up
groceries, befuddled.
I dash to the washed chicken
as it thaws in disquietude
to season it with the spice of propaganda.
Then, I let it marinate in ginger garlic,
slathering layers of barbecue sauce,
until the elements soak in
their hostility tenderized.
I condemn the importance of stereotypes
acknowledging their hype,
I place my misgivings each of them deftly
onto the skewers
basting them in blobs of indulgence
into butter bubbles melting away
my fears roasting on the spit fire.
I hum a dirge in this awakening,
dusting off the crumbs that lie
in the rotisserie of my delusions-
scarred, charred and marred
on iron bars.

SOIREES
(Inspired by Fitzgerald's, 'The Great Gatsby')

The Jazz age soirees always had
a well- stocked cellar of liquor
some even contraband,
Viscous bubbles, floating citrusy kites
laced with streaks of grenadine
and ice marbles, plenty of them to dress up a banquet.
Spruced with lime, crème de cassis
and club soda- indispensable for all drinks.

Swirling in the decadence
of the intoxicant bursting through
the caved walls of his mouth,
he could always still taste her
on his tongue as Daisy slept on his lids,
Drunk with passion of a whorish night,
he awaited another sunrise
to wash down this hangover.

a parenthesis
of a careless hangover
drunk on musings.

THE LOVE AFFAIR

My memory train chugs, puffing out a clear day,
Its silken strands – cerulean blue and salmon hued
slither into my consciousness
unbolting my caged dreams.
My splintered freedom breathes at last
through valves of hope and certainty.
Time's winkles filigreed on its metal frame
weave a montage of images, life's cruel game-
Scrunched paper balls, masks, Amazon deliveries,
reprogrammed work schedules, the online drudgery
are now uninstalled from my memory.

Surrogacy has burst its waters, drifting me
from braided metal bars into open sky.
The blustery wind caresses my longings,
Its feathery fingers spooning mouthfuls of
splattered lush green valleys, carmine buds
and wrinkled peaks carpeted with fresh snow.
Skeleton boughs erupt with dawn's murmur,
Scented damask roses and jasmine
waft through my olfactory senses
and I breathe their intoxicating perfume.

My city melts its hostility and breathes too
draping its sensuousness with air curtains.
I am swept in its strong gust - swishing, swirling,
sussurating through the predicament of leaves,
misty window panes and dregs of despair.

I breathe in the fragrances of blossoming trails
the fire crackling up a lively chatter,
the mellowness of coffee brewing in a neighbour's kitchen,
the petrichor that languorously creeps into my sinuses
and as I revive them all, the love affair continues.

A NEW DAWN

Lungs of my cityscape inhale tender yearnings
of a new dawn, fluttering on wings.
Smoke rings circle her blue veined fingers
and vanish into the ghostly night.
The tree silhouetting the baya weaver's nest
ruffles its emerald flags,
Dulcet melodies orbit the amaltas
wafted by the breath of Spring.
Feathery fingers levitate my spirits,
interlocking them in its embrace.

I breathe 'Amen!' - rebooting my world,
salvaging it from the hollow dankness of gloom.
I delete plastic smiles, unlock the password to freedom
flying grey pigeons through open dormer roofs.
I paste my tangerine sun back in the sky,
filtering the unchained particles of happiness.
No stocking up supplies nor bitter pills dunked
No oxygen concentrators to be the only lifeline,
Sidewalks bustle with enthusiasm now
Buses filling up hoards of scurrying passengers.
What separated them, binds them now
in molecules of its billowing embrace.
The air flutters into butterflies, to dusk, to cotton clouds
to men that vanish to dust but momentarily
only to be breathed back to life again, 'Amen!'

THOSE RED TULIPS

Mornings are the best time of the day. A cup of tea
poured out from a kettled sun, its searing energy
framing my window. I let it toast my skin, melting it a bronze-
like Buddha in my living room, squatting on a frayed
laced runner wearing a tuliped grin. Is it a reminder of sorts?

I do my chores, run the washing machine, cook, clean,
put on my Sunday best, my body- a battlefield
lips pouting red to shift the attention from a lacerated wrist.
The altar has fresh tulips, redder than the scars sitting in
hospital rooms, against dull white walls, mourning
life and its losses therein.
The redder they grow, I become suspicious of their lips-
blood red did she describe them or cold in her veins after death?

I buy tulips as a present for a friend, disappointed because
they don't smell like jasmines or violets or hyacinths.
If they smelled good, would they bring rubies on her cheeks,
Or would her hands reek of blood again, dipped in Dior?
I remember the night he made love to her
He brought me tulips of the very same kind,
We strung them around our necks and imagined
We wore a new skin of rubies, not the bronze I now own.

Didn't they smell numb then or was it the medicines?
Her laughter echoed and all I could see was tulips
Splattered on the floor. The gun had misfired-
No, she wasn't to rest in the tulips- it was a mistake.

MY ROOTS

A tiara embellishes nature's crown
melting the shackled past with its aura.
The ambrosial Ganga and Saraswati our sorrows drown
paying obeisance to the land I proudly call my own.
A paean for the blessings showered won't suffice,
Oh, beacon of light to the world unknown.

Truth flows on scented shikaras and palanquins as zealous lips
curl
to croon an anthem that envisions timeless virtues
of towering Himalayas and Vindhyas that adorn your neck
with pearls
Steeped in culture rich as wealthy Croesus accrues
a saga of bravery and martyrdom unfurls.
Oh, land of our forefathers, martyrs and minstrels.

Wreaths of marigold and champa deck your deities
wafting the air with mellow fragrance
while banyan, gulmohar and pines skirt lush valleys
weaving your emerald tapestry with their magnificence,
My heart envisions this fabric of prosperity.
Oh, beauteous land of exquisite charm and radiance.

The brooch of conviction proudly hemmed on your sleeve
embraces diverse races, religions and creeds
celebrating Holi, Id and Lohri each with flavours unique
Humanity and hospitality of Nawabs are cornerstones
the world emulates and from your ripe breasts receives,
Oh, freedom and respect always you enthrone.

India my Kohinoor and pride
An eagle's eye cannot fathom your sincerity
Pinions soar proclaiming granthas you abide
Wise sages chant your bhajans with sanctity,
Every inch of soil nurtured and hallowed
Oh yes, with blood, tears and humility.

A land where corruption is vanquished completely
Education is imparted and not just a degree,
Where Kathak and Kuchipudi express more than words,
No groveling for favours or fake sympathy
traditions crocheted with henna and saffron threads
Oh, mighty India my golden bird.

Creativity blossoms in your ethereal wings
from quills of Tagore and Sarojini Naidu.
Music encompassing strains of divinity springs
from maestros like Pandit Ravi Shankar and Ustaad Zakir
Hussain
who sparkle in a star spangled sky your praises to sing
Oh, India the bedrock of music and poetry.

Nestled between Arabian sea and Indian ocean,
the exotic flora thrives in your abundance
and women like Goddess Durga are adulated with devotion.
No wars emanating through hate or dissension
And peace, technology and medicine are given attention.
Oh, India my motherland, this is the future I anticipate.

IN THE STILL OF THE NIGHT
(A Ghazal)

Time wilts away its purple glow silently in the still of night
as the brow of night wanes gently in the still of night.

A nightingale trills a mellifluous melody
as the plangent river flows tremulously in the still of the night.

Clouds weep tears for the one I loved
as dreams melt away treacherously in the still of night.

Cypress and columbine cannot run thorns deeper
into a heart shattered by a beloved mercilessly in the still of
night.

The sea swells its melancholic waves
to thrust them upon her shore so perfidiously in the still of
night.

My heart beckons the moonlight fervently
to steal a kiss and on his heart engrave it slowly in the still of
night.

The mist of memories will haunt me evermore
as their drops caress my soul tenderly in the still of night.

I pine for my love on the other shore
wiping my pain that flows incessantly in the still of night.

Seek I not broken dreams that breathe unkind
or deception that lurks in shrouds surreptitiously in the still of
night.

Unspoken words echo, binding us forever in eternity's harness
where no one else can keep us apart cruelly in the still of night.

MY IDENTITY- MY NAME

When heavy lidded winter beamed its resplendence,
a stork nested on roofs of primal anxiety expectantly
popping a tiny princess with hazelnut eyes blinking bashfully,
Rapturous joy erupted, marvelling at God's magnificence.

Names crept from purple petal lips, dew kissed that crisp eve-
ning
a few soaked their delicate wings in dappled December sun,
Some flitted and warbled in her little basinet for fun
while a poet said, "Our birth is but a sleep and a forgetting."

Ten long springs they waited for her to unfurl her wings
Forget- me-nots would soon sprout in the garden of the Liddle's
Two pouted lips babbling away a string of puzzling riddles
'Candy,', 'our precious,' were endearments that would soon ring.

Finally, a name folded itself in an ethereal embrace
welcoming the 'beautiful angel' flapping her wings to unfold
letters of wizened folk engraved in gold,
Songs of exultation wove the air with love's crocheted lace.

Leaves rustled their strings to whisper 'Vandita!' lovingly.
As the wind tweaked her cotton cheeks in gentle approval
Her childish prattle, gibberish chatter and foozle
curled into their hearts, nestling there permanently.

THE MIST

We leave our longings
in palms of a dappled dawn.
in the mist of a forest's frown
in the crackle of warm winter twigs.
December rolls her carpet in, yet unsurely,
diamond coronets drape the severed pine knolls.
My train to Shimla rumbles in, screeching to a halt
Heavy with musk of the Shivalik range, it empties itself
onto the waiting platform, gulping in passengers by the dozen.
Two men roll their wheeled suitcases and pot bellies in
A vendor thrusts in a few cups of tea, Twirling its
spicy flavours through the open window, I sit through it all
the whistle, whirring of its engine, waving hands- a blur.
The train chugs out following my gaze, following the trees
that stand to whispering attention in the breeze.
We cross Kalka, a wooden bridge, one of the many 800
during our journey. There is no haste so we prefer the toy train
or so it's called, instead of just driving down five hours straight.
The boughs hang with perfume and possibilities
Memories of sojourns we had hoped to take
And some that we did embark upon
Would he be waiting at the next hairpin bend
where the air almost sucks you in
where breath is no longer mist?
Words haunt the monolith of my thoughts
where cavernous membranes are riddled with memories.
This must be the last halt I tell myself-
Am I the sojourner here?
Let's do something quirky, perhaps, a freefall
Then will the mist cover me too?

NATURE'S GEM

She is nature's spark lighting up the heavens-
a tear in God's own eyes,
Infusing mirth to a world devoid of it.
Created from man's rib,
the whole universe radiates her charm.
An alluring smile that makes flowers bloom
and sweet nightingales sing
Such is her aura.
A diamond that adorns many a home,
 she illuminates with her sparkle.
Cocooned in her nest, lie her little ones
imbibing values that she acquaints them with.
A gentle touch, a soft voice
Ah! feels the pain of others
welling up in her eyes,
She absorbs and assimilates
all that is true and wise
and blesses all her progeny.
If patience could be personified
or compassion brought to life
If love could be defined,
it only and only will seek habitation
in the soul of a woman.

EERIE ENCOUNTERS

Pancakes, honey and cinnamon doughnuts
were laced with some sizzling conversation,
Lanterns guided their road with sharp cuts
All set for a sinfully gluttonous vacation.

The motel opened on a desolate bend
So, they checked in for a siesta
Not a soul stirred, no sign nor board
The manager said, "Hasta la vista."

The raven sky pasted a silver orb on their window
while somewhere, an owl hooted loud and clear
They heard the wind howl, it began to snow
and in their closet, wailing they could hear.

The door creaked and something stirred
They were locked inside in the blizzard.

DÉJÀ VU

Spring erupts with fistfuls of sunshine,
The breeze a flutter of birds trilling sonatas
on verdant branches, thawing
the aching silence of a winter's embrace
over peaks laden with snow.

Those frolicking bursts of joy
Fling me into reminiscences of childhood-
moist feet pattering on soft sand
when the wind chased us into caves
our echoes ricocheting in their dank walls.

The sea washed our ruddy faces,
drenching our clothes in its sweetness
Squirrels nibbled on cloven chestnuts
scurrying about. My legs, a highway of bones
Dangling over sun kissed rocks.

Purple lilacs still bloom there
with the aromatic fragrance of June,
In crimson corners of my heart
nestles the flame of the forest,
igniting my rapturous déjà vu.

THE TREE WITH A FAMILIAR SCENT

There's a teak tree in the tropical forest
that has sprouted roots in me.
Often, I see my blue veins throbbing
with their viscous sap - the blue
of the ocean that washes
the rough particles off my hands
when I trace patterns on the semolina
sitting in a bowl beside me,
the canvas of my watered dreams.
Once a reality, gone in a fleeting moment
washed away, swept in my misty eyes
that reflect the anguish of the moaning wind
brushing through brambles and bushes
in an avalanche. Those cacophonous echoes
against the cliffs are my mournful dreams
truncated like the tree I knew by its familiar scent.
Its sandpaper trunk where I yearned to rest,
its leathery scent that I ached for always
I sit on my coffee table strumming
on the wood where birds once sat
now a stump, the branches have vanished
and so, have the birds.
I am the tree and the tree is within me.

THE ENCHANTRESS

The nimbus azure swirls ambrosial charms
melting his thoughts into myriad velvet hearts
that splatter and patter like the first summer rain.
There against the errant sky
she unrobes her sensuality
is she real or just his fantasy?

She unfurls her petalled lips
to kiss fairy dreams that are hers
those he had nurtured with his tears.
The sussurous leaves capture the enigma
of her lingering fragrance
for she pirouettes on them each night
before the hush gives way to morning chatter.

She is the enchanting zephyr swaying
to a rhapsody of the celestial spheres
clothed in argent robes,
frisking her black tresses of night
catching dewdrops trickling down her bosom.
Will he succumb to the sublunary passion
her moonbeam eyes ignite?

She is the red rose dipping her wings
on a wine kissed branch,
as she sinks her thorns into his heart
on a ripe night when the caterpillar
morphs into an exquisite butterfly.

BONHOMIE

Permafrost stiffens its layered embrace
thawing, crumbling into an avalanche
then in the blink of an eye gone
Gone in a vaporous haze - a trumpet sounds
drowning the cacophony in whirlpools of froth.
The opaque stillness of night slinks through a mercurous dawn
unfurling its crimson petals in the azure,
Dappled silhouettes cavort to the symphony of
disarming delusions in outgrown parasols.
sloshed with amber kisses on velvet lips,
The blue jacaranda by the window
still holds a withered sway
for the charcoal night has gone up in fumes.
Its white icy fangs swallowing the pine knolls,
combing their fronds back into my palm
that now drill another story, trill a song
from a repertoire of the Northern folk lore.
A pregnant silence breathes her sensuous drops,
peeling winter off my skin
as hope envelops in chortles, whistling
a new song of peace and bonhomie.

A LOST CAUSE

Cardamom eyes dim their shutters
as another day hems to a close gently
in the echoing strains of a songbird.
Its trill sits upon the twilight haze
in the breath rasping in my chest
awakening mercurial drops of solitude
to drench tarantula thoughts-
Muddled, befuddled in an hourglass
where a fire dies in the throbbing veins
of an autumn night still suckling
on maple leaves with withered breasts,
bleeding woes into gravitational inconstancy
of the moon's repressive tact.
In affirmations of another bid to retract,
it waxes into a fulness
imprinting scars of another winter
treading on rustic dreams, stifling
enmeshed in nets of a forgotten tide.
The tide that only returns its dead
to a watery bedrock of algae,
in colours of bronze, coal and pewter grey
while the sun filters through their eyes
now rocks- cold and transfixed
covered in the shroud of a misnomer.
The fire doused in their wombs
The abode for aborted dreams, some stillborn
snuffed out in the smoke of a lost cause
drifting into the inevitability of death's jaws.

THE MONTAGE

I have sized up the weeds
in empty corners of my life,
in what lies within and without,
in the sifting and incipient drifting of dry debris
on a palm filching, crushing together memories of the past
stubborn dog-eared pages refusing to budge.
Now bursts open a montage of images, desecrating
the lattice of my overgrown solace where rests a shovel
to snip off Spear thistles unwanted, those
that germinate into biennial cycles.
Nascent fires crackle up again
carried in the fennel's stalk by P.
Halogen eyes blink through dark tunnels
where Oizys holds sway
slithering through pockets torn with strife
drenched in sweat, they submerge into brine
Eyelids - a containment zone of mortified fears
Who's life is it I wonder?
I look at empty shells streaked with blood
and the nascent dripping from my eyes.
The dog-eared pages demystified
haunt me invasively, I am tongue tied
for they are spilt into an ether womb
into a million split images they float
Then and now, the time we lived
I thrust those visages in a thresh
stoking the woodfire in my grate
to burn the weeds they contain.

THE NON-EXISTENT IDENTITY

I slink away into binaries
The real and the acquired
Truth and illusion,
Known and unknown,
Native and alien,
stiff as a cancan dress unworn.
My fingers slipping into numerals
Variables- denoting a notation system.
Counting and uncounting,
Forgetting and recounting,
deciphering the matrix of my life trapped
in equations of X and Y, chromosomes chaotically entrapped
between what is or should have been
between the here and the now;

Before the sun rests its burnished petals
on my ghosted landscape,
                    I ask – [Why?]

Why myriad chants echo in my zendo,
those memories- now barbed wires of prejudice
crisscross lines run riot in my mind.
While a sentinel lamppost squints
blinding those numbers away,
leaving me at the mercy of shadows unkind
compassing them into cambered walls
of my mind.
I scratch the parenthesis off the wreath

That blurs numbers etched beneath,
Those fated numbers haunt me again
dew drops that scratch my windowpane.
The hexagonal patterns on my yoga mat
trace an opacity into my hologram smile,
dislodging my apprehensions
furrowing my diasporic identity.
I count caterpillar lines that make no sense now
I slink into the backwaters of a past legacy
no longer mine=
A cipher, a nadir, a non-existent me.

SHOWERS OF LOVE

Its two am and the fire needs tending,
The air is heavy with jasmine.
Ripened in a longing, a clock ticks
to the rustle of autumn's swell.

No visitor called today, not even blackbirds
Only the rusty creak of the door, unlatched
and the piercing draughts crept in,
flexing their way to keep her company.

She holds a raindrop in her palm
to savour his fragrance still warm,
Old melodies take wing in her heart
of initials untraced on her spangled wrist.

Her breath grows weak, the fight is o'er
No task undone, she has nought to gain.
There is the hum of winter's chill
in the solitude of a night's refrain.

THE TREACHEROUS MANDREL

A firefly flits with
psychedelic dreams woven on a mandrel,
I am told the lady who spins silver yarn
draws them back on threads of purple ermine.
Then on an ebony night when the moon is a longan,
the wind hovers between velutinous cascades,
unleashing an avalanche, masking her tears,
her incomprehensible fears
that nestle in petals
of white gold, her soul,
hushing the gravity of her moans.

Her broken heart- a volcano
erupting with pearls from her
kohl rimmed dewy eyes.
They blanket her joys
fading them from existence,
fading away from reality
into the cacophony of a fierce night,
dousing it into smoke
of an airplane's trail.

Yet dawn dries her dreams
in the parturient belly of the azure
streaked in her ripened hair,
the reflection of the night
silvered and waning into grey
until the mandrel weaves in a frenzy
and
a thread breaks...
[in her soul.]

A NEW IDENTITY

I transcend binaries- real and acquired,
Clutching hemispheres of creeds
in cobbled pathways ensconced.
My apprehensions in an orhni wrapped
reflect its myriad hues in my eyes,
hope braided along the nape of my neck
and tattooed in my veins.
Fingers morph into numerals
unconstrained by ethnocentrism
unsealed in equations of identity.
Petals of my being burnished by an alien sun
on a distant landscape. I introspect, 'Is this me?'
A myriad shlokas echo my sensibilities
congregating into memories, both native and alien.
While these identities merging together,
a sentinel lamppost squints
blinding those numbers away
leaving me at the confluence
of a new culture poised at the threshold.
I scratch the parenthesis off the slate
smudging my apprehensions.
Those fated numbers dauntless again
scratch my windowpane in a dewy mist
a hybrid consciousness blurs
in the hologram of my mind.

Those caterpillar lines on snow paved streets
Carry me into backwaters of my past.

No longer am I constrained by a sufi's chant
nor complacent in the dust of my ancestral legacy
A new identity stitches into folds of my skin,
I feel the call of humanity that comforts me
in its warm embrace, divorced from the din.

(First published in SETU magazine, Feb, 2020)

AN AUTUMNAL NIGHT

Cardamom lids dim their shutters
as another day hems to a close- gently, purposefully,
in the echoing strains of a songbird.
Its trill sits upon the twilight haze
in the breath rasping in my chest
or the warm mercurial drops of solitude
that drench tarantula thoughts.
Muddled, befuddled in an hourglass
a fire dies in the throbbing
of an autumnal night, still suckling
on maple leaves with withered breasts
bleeding its woes into gravitational allegiance.
Hastening infringements to retract
the moon's repressive act
of waxing to a fulness
or imprinting footsteps of a hostile winter
that treads on dampened dreams,
Stifled in nets of a forgotten tide-
the tide that only returns its dead
to a watery bedrock of algae,
in dreadful bronze, coal and pewter grey.
The sea is their abode for dreams,
a womb birthing the stillborn
aborted in rivers – bleeding, breathing.
While the sun filters through lids
rock cold in comatose, it glimmers
covered in the shroud of a misnomer
stretching, straining to resurface.

(First published in SETU Magazine, Pittsburg, U.S.A. Feb, 2020)

THE BIRTH OF A POEM

In the viscosity of a mother's womb
stirrings of a poem are felt,
Germinating from the coitus of words-
a creation, fusion of mind and soul
intermingling in a rhythmic cadence.
Nourished through the umbilical cord
which nurtures its form into an embryo.
The amniotic fluid facilitating, inking
transmission of the unwritten words
onto the tapestry of the muse's mind.
Poised with each contraction, the foetus
Outward is thrust into a chaotic world
Ever hopeful for its birth/ death
Marking its identity on virgin paper.

A symbiotic bond
Of mind and soul
Until waters burst.

LIFE IN MONOCHROME

Time for the school bus
[It's 7 am] already
and hands tick tock in my brain.
Slipping back/ away- echoing
a rumble of unfamiliar voices
sauntering past the tin shack
with boisterous steps across the asphalt.
Lizards, mice, mosquitoes and men
All surfacing and resurfacing
Some tawny and freckled, others fidgety
grunting guttural/ squeaky sounds.
Two jingling bellies,
[one balancing an aquiline nose],
count anthills of nickels- no time to lose.
A lad twirls around smoke circled
tables, setting and unsetting them, muttering-

No money,
No food!
They vanish in smoke.

Another withered hand scrubs grime off cars
that drone off on the silken ribbon,
Crouching between neon eyes- the traffic buzz
a woman grapples for a crutch
or sometimes her shawl, the clattering bowl-
her wretched hearing aid,
where did they all go?

A cart trundles on- ahead/ into the dust
yet something breaks the din.
The singularity of silence-
a life in monochrome.

The school bus finally emerges
hurtling visages away into dust
Perhaps to birth as blossoms
in another season.

TIME'S FILIGREE

In the trellis where the wind sweeps,
A cuckoo's hush gently creeps
nestling words in a lush foliage-

Milk rivers flow
from lightning scarred skies
streaked with blood.

Crimping this garland of inked gems
into a filigree of time's wounds
on twilight's crepuscule breast-

Old rusty wheels
the lumberjack's craft
crumbling time to teak again.

CARPE DIEM
(Inspired by J.M. Synge's play, 'Riders to the Sea')

In the morass of a decaying day
knotted reeds swell into serpents.

The tide turns a monster
tugging at all that's left –
Michael, Bartley and the other progeny

swallowed up, ferrying dreams
on white halter-less horses.

They rode in these verdant climes,
five men of Maurya's family
until roses replaced thorns
and lashing shards their hopes,
washing their carcasses up/ out
to the white rocks by the sea.

The heart of a mother cold
whispering benedictions
no more. Until -
          [the cross stood alone]
in mute reverence
and moonbeams filtered through
the chalice of suffering.
It is finished-
This too shall pass
Each day is a Carpe Diem.

STILL FAMILIAR

We scrambled away
Into the dense forest, he and I,

Our teens swallowed by
summer's searing tongue.

I often chased birds, perched
on hollow skeletons-

Overhanging creepers bearded in
a dank embrace, their names

I don't recall. Green silhouettes hooding
slivers of light dotting our ruddy palms.

He inched closer to his fate, I tried to stop him
But he paid no heed, my heart

numbed by a cold refrain, I called him
by another name, in another time and place.

His voice still familiar, but I couldn't recall
the name nor face.

One day into the fateful haze he tread
where the silvery moon stopped dead.

The front-page news read-
An Unidentified Body Surfaces in the River
"Twenty-four and counting,"
his mother still proudly said.

MY OWN STORY

I live in three bubbles now- two make believe
collapsing before me like a newspaper,
Through headlines, I skim:
"The lockdown is extended till July 31st," Who cares?
Another one mentions an upsurge
in insurgencies, homicides, earthquakes and floods,
Life is a haze in the synapse of my brain
It's trials- an aching cough that continues to persist.

I pen a valedictory speech for a friend today
But ironically, my own blood splatters
across white crumpled sheets.
Twenty- five years to have laboured in an organization,
Yes, you heard right,
Twenty- five staggering years of fear and failure
I tried peeling them off my hands.
But they stick like bubble-gum,
an astringent rubs them clean now
but the dust has settled in my nails
refusing to be dislodged. I still recollect
the catatonic whirring of the drilling machine
which still jars in my ears until I'm tone deaf
It drills black holes in my brain.
Chalk particles slink into my eyes
impaling my retina-
strapped to a voiceless chant
refurbishing a laboured breath.

Teaching sans eyes and ears has become habitual
I teach in my sleep, ranting philosophies
of Plato, Aristotle and others I forget now.
Immersed in an ocean of thought,
my head reels with numbers, names and theories.
"Out, out brief candle!" echoes aloud in my ears.

I hear the clamouring again, this time of comrades
Am I hallucinating or insane?
"Get away you!" I beseech.
Hoards stalk me like ants poised for a kill
Crawling up my arm, chewing lifeless fingers
marmalade pulpy now.
All vanish like a nightmare
no ants anymore to navigate my thoughts.
All I hear is a ghostly wind tapping at my door
And murky shadows of have beens and had beens
creeping into cadavers of splintered time.

A TRIBUTE TO THE GANGES

Pools of undiluted mirth
Butterfly days, a childhood smeared in sunshine
on my vermilion ribboned forehead.
Dhols of Spring beckoning pattering feet
towards the soulful chants of 'Om.'
My boat eyes paying obeisance to your grandeur
carelessly draped in a viridian dhoti, the creases
speckled with cobalt ruffles, bathing my tawny skin.
Smothered in your tresses I would often lie,
rolling my fingers gently across them, sharing innocent secrets
playfully sipping a warmth drenched in your frowns and
smiles.

The network of your reptilian cobalt veins
marble cold, throbbing in tandem with mine –
reminders of the time I played on your dark-skinned banks
until the maturing sun burnished your opalescent lips.
Frosty sighs of achromatic gloom settling at the nape of your
neck
making inroads deep into your womb
scarred by mortal lust, seeping in mercilessly.
Leaden clouds paled into sunken cheekbones
when you gurgled the froth of human transgression
purged in your ever- encompassing embrace.

Twenty years ago, I rowed through your wrinkled visage
Summer conches welcomed another season
stringing marigold beads in your tresses.
My oars suckled your watery breasts

tinkling your anklets mischievously.
"Maa, forgive me," I said.
Your unbridled tempest joyously pelting braids of blessings.

that bridge between us had broken in the deluge-

Today, I ink you into parchment skin
Combing back those raven tresses
dishevelled but not fossilized by time or distance
into postcard memories.
Rajnigandha kisses mist my glass panes,
Yet, my children's paper boats I pray
will flow you back someday.

LET'S PLAY A GAME

Let's play, animating ashen brows suspended above silvery
wisps of lace
Or on Eagle winged chariots, tracing toes above the cumulous,
casting a hypnotic spell
Your breath alive, spewing serpents on my windowpane, our
misty solitude.

The ocean untamed mounted by the sickle moon scatters
splinters of light-
Clustered orbs flaunting sportively their silver lustred nails
illuminate the azure,
Yonder Jasmine lips sip honeyed dew, intoxicating the
cobwebbed, waxen night as this.

Lush green meadows decked with Spring diadems, heartily trill
a chorus of Nightingale songs,
Moths flitting in a euphoric maze make the air heavy with
dulcet melodies swirling echoes of a lapping brook in the
ravine.
Nightbirds coo, making amorous advances, bathing under a
naked moonlight.

We are driftwood wading on the tousled sheet of pitch black,
you and I,
I write your name a million times conjuring up rosebuds on
your dimpled cheeks,
Two lanterns ablaze in your kohled eyes, wash away the
gathering gloom.

The chordophone sitting upon my knee, plays you in its pizzica-
to quavers
Tugging your heartbeats to my bosom, sweat tides break over
my wrinkled forehead,
Our bodies heaving, surging into a deep cloud of smoke
Until we become a chariot- thrusting, slithering, loosening the
reins that bind us.

The rein snaps, swallowing you into its wheels, a trap, shedding
off beetle skin
A charcoal door unhinges into the cosmos as the dregs of
quietude vanish,
Sipping off remaining sighs congregated in my cup, I strum
along as the bagatelle ends.

A HAIBUN: MONSTERS UNDER THE BED

Night slips into a tar can, pasting a moon above my window-
pallid, silvery, white. My carousel head spinning bucket-lists,
manoeuvring caterpillar lines, scuttling through a barrage of
quizzical glances sizing me up, pot-bellied shoves - a Silicon
world of porcelain faces, heavy jawed men and women glaring
menacingly at my coppery velvet skin, burnished in the sun.
The Green Chartreuse and Toccata and Fugue in D minor
linger on my lips like his kiss last night when his heart
shuttered its windows forever. No conjuring up our devils, no
running fingers down neck contours, thrusting skin, erupting
in an avalanche of emotions lying spent on silken sheets,
swirling fork tongues, playing hide and seek, tasting
passion- now cold and lifeless in a crumpled heap.

Finally, back to my comfort zone, my home (for decades), the
mind is still a whirlwind, a volcano, a monster seething with
revenge. Alone, the fugitive me, reclaims the glass menagerie,
my world of unicorns and rag dolls. Fragile, shattered yet still
mine. I satiate the gluttonous night snowballing his
memorabilia- old moth-eaten love letters, round trip air tickets,
crunched up outstanding credit card bills and cobwebbed gift
wrappers. They hang origami coffins in the under belly of my
box bed.
Tugging a crucifix against my breast- the icicles melt, I shed
off the scales, cross my heart, chuckling: "No horned creatures
with fangs and forked tongues will stir tonight!" I roll into an
Armadillo ball, heavy lidded, comatose like sleep.
Crimson lips surfeit
Pieces of succulent meat
I toast to their death.

THE LAZY MUSIC IS STILL

Spring is in the air, billowing melodies from a misty conch
Shafts of tangerine wash dewy diamonds off serrated leaves,
rustling on knobbly Cypress benches.
Nascent groves of warted Hedgehog chestnuts ripen, tangoing
in misty parasols of carmine blush,
Their spiny burrs threshing moss green wisps, blanketing the
undergrowth,
Sticky sepia blood like sap drips across skeletal branches, tip
toeing on the emerald crusted canopy
The Weeping Willow sweeps the river bank, scattering lush
green diadems bleached in amber glaze, exfoliating tanned flesh
of pregnant earth.

Come summer and fiery vermilion strands spear through
nature's tapestry, weaving webbed green-lipped wattle shrubs
on its aromatic bed,
Honey syrup squirts filtering through my tepid hands hollowed
into a heart, birthing goldfish sparks.
Chiseling feathery sculptors, woodpeckers drill their bills into
hoary arms of the birch –drumming notes in its hollow womb
to unearth larvae nests
Leaves of Wattle shrubs sprout gold bangled blossoms swaying
in the searing heat
The Caribou brush their coal clumped antlers against the birch,
devouring velvet blackberries in a succulent abandon.
Wispy mosses sprouting silver flecked green catkins oasis the
hope of a peaceful reverie as silver belled asters, powdered with
tinkling moondust sprinkle confetti across the sky,

But hark! No more is the trill heard. Fossilized in the vagaries
of time, these dollops of butter-scotch sun fade with the
summer
For the avalanche of hard crusted, heavy boned winter -oars its
silver sequined boat to stay.
Resilient, red berried, spindly Junipers comb across the
cottoned quietude
Ornately rich, yet the marble filigreed brook mirrors a
sepulchral silence,
Slowly waves recede to a lull, their lethargic ragas slink into the
conch
Earmarking the day when an arthritic limbed forest will rest
until Spring bursts again.

A METAMORPHOSIS

Life breathed in parchment skin, a book - its leaves now lifeless, fossilized in
the sands of time
A boy sits atop his charred apple globe, a canon-ball chair -his microcosm,
trying to decipher spidery letters through a loupe.
The convex ray convergence has charred the letters into smoky carcasses,
His borrowed eyes -the lens magnifies his nigrified world, dusting its hues on him.

Then, his body undergoes a metamorphosis, lost wax casting, polishing in the kiln,
Patina with its final touches preserving him from corrosion/ weathering.
Now searching for answers, he introspects: Why? Why did the myopic world melt within his veins, their ashen beliefs?
Why was his bronze skin burnished with scars of an earlier time/ place?

In his parchment pleats, letters unfold, strangers- staring at him punctuated by the parentheses of his mind.
No longer can his winged dreams be entrapped in sprawling letters of a book
No longer his visage will wear a leaden look
His kite dreams will soar high above nimbus clouds on the golden sill.

The bulle of his mind inflates, encompassing a universe larger
than the midget globe he sits on,
His life books flutters into a flag in his hands victoriously.
Blood gushing through his veins, his leathery mates ready to
stride 'the road less travelled.'
Bubbles refracting rainbow colours float across his mindscape,
inking dreams through pores of papery skin.
Those dreams have broken through the delusive watery,
charcoal frame,
Flapping into golden fireflies, washing the macrocosm with
renewed hope.

SEASONS

Seasons always change, but why, I wonder?
The fireball dips, cracking arteries of azure
with the momentum of a shepherd's crook
thrusting its spears into vermilion May's sighs.

An unwelcome June sputters its zest
across heaven's bed in a feverish fret
at the cusp of birthing, un-birthing, rebirthing
a dappled July in the womb of its death.

Fissured ruby lips writhing, rumbling
accords July a diamond crusted welcome,
A cavalcade of purple men oar June back
to its wrinkled sand dunes.

"Criquet—croquet,' chirp the crickets
while buds wave their wings, dripping,
fluttering over my palm, fragrant
musings silhouetted in silken nimbus.

Leggy rhododendrons preen their regalia-
my head resting against a clump, unlearning Homer.
recalling the sights and sounds of Mumbai especially the rain
funneling out its fragrances through my pores.

DEAD SILENCES

Bubbles rise in the dark waters
Filtering light through limpid skin.

I'm reminded of a wharf, there the
fisherman often prepare their nets, until

the azure settles its crimson fins
on the tide, rising and falling-

Nets cast each day hold trout sinfully
in blue serpentine tongues.

Fibres of azure unhooking
their silences into the ocean.

It is not the bubbles anymore
nor the spools of the fishing rod,

Perhaps it is my eyes that
see what is to be seen-

An ocean rolling itself, hiding
its secrets, frothing into bubbles.

The Trade winds dispelling darkness
throbbing in veins of the ocean.

Hope's bubbles are the first to burst.

GREY CLOUDS
A Micro poem

Grey clouds unhinge,
bleeding into letters
of a wistful night untamed
all that's left are dregs-
coffee, music, petrichor
in a waning moon's sigh
shrouded in the kohl of sky.

ROSEATE SONNETS
(A sonnet form pioneered by Dr. Koshy A.V.)

The Ice Maiden

Frozen days melted as ice,
slowly dripping ditties
infused the maiden's mind
with profound curiosity.

Seasons eclipsed her radiance
bashfully mystical,
Her beauty unsurpassed
reflected a temper so mercurial.

As tides ebbed, the moon waned
her presence passively restrained.

Rendering help, she strode
Oblivious to envy's glowering eyes,
She stumbled on her fateful journey
Etched on a deserted tombstone.

(First published in The Roseate Sonnets Anthology, 2020)

THE SCIENCE OF NOT KNOWING
(To a grandmother who once loved me)

It grew from misplaced memories,
alphabets, silhouettes, a broken thread
dusting her day off in sighs.
And so, my grandma lived many lives.

Today she calls me by another name, the real one
lost to half- truths or so I pretend, the drone
reels on, when she hums a familiar song
resonating from voices in her head.

She connects the dots but they punctuate her sky
with tears, yet she smiles living the lie.

Ruthless flashes appear treacherously
On the periphery of dementia.
Since not knowing has become a habit now
Ever so common with her these days.

BLUE ROSES
(Inspired from Tennessee Williams, 'The Glass Menagerie')

It's a cold glassy night, I slink into bed
Clouds draping my window and hers.
No, not curtains, pray how would the glass be visible
Or would it be, except a bit more vulnerable?

So, sits her vulnerability in the glass unicorn
It sat 'blue roses' for years or were they pink,
pink as the brace she wore on her leg that chased
gentlemen callers away or was it her paranoia?

Vulnerability is now long forgotten
It exists only in the real world of men.

Roses are always blue not red in my world
Of glass figurines and illusions,
Sometimes these illusions break into shards
Each mirroring our destiny.

THE SNOW GIRL
(Inspired by an old Russian tale)

Rolled from spring, burnished by the sun
Hopped a girl of snow if ever there was one,
Her childless parents created her from a snowball
She supplanted happiness in their lives in the fall.

The solstice of spring gave her wings
So off she went berry picking in a dense forest.
Carrying a basket full of hope and undiluted mirth
Scrambling off tenaciously with her friends.

"Haloo!" howled the Bear in vile curiosity
"Haloo!" growled Grey wolf in the garb of felicity.

Resilient, she paid no heed to their pleas,
Only on Zhuchka's call she clambered down.
Skulked the wolf with a deep-seated frown
Envying the victory nature had sown.

THE RIVER

The river meanders, carrying fragrances
shedding skin of a hostile winter,
Tossed from its source like cobble stones
men ride its waves on flower decked boats.

Sometimes, dawn weaves vignettes of a blue epicurean
as it bustles with children, sinuous arms flexing
It becomes a hundred chameleons, changing colours with time
from emerald to amber to pewter grey then back to emerald.

Calcified in a mountain's breast, its milk seeps,
threading through sentinel pines of a sylvan deep.

Ruminating possibilities of an idyllic setting
Or suckling in the inebriated enigma of Beethoven
Sensuously, I inhale its fragrance – fresh and warm
Earthed in blood, pulsing through papered veins.

WHEATFIELD WITH CROWS
(Inspired by a painting by Van Gogh)

Come golden spring, fields smear streaks
of mosaic tapestry, charcoaled wings immerse
their brows of grief in sodden straw heads waving,
shrugging the silver scythe hanging in the blue overhead.

Those harbingers swoop brazenly stringing
ominous secrets, pollinating death but hope still glistens
on goldfish backs against cobalt wrinkles- a night's embers
Parrot ribbons smolder in fire tongues lashing them.

Leopards run amok in gold flecked catharsis
mulling over this legerity in its caryopsis.

Ripened grain endless fissures, embracing,
Outsourcing colours from bleeding palettes,
Squawking crows canvassed into ebony clusters
Etching an impasto of sustained hopelessness.

EAU DE VIE NIGHTS
(A tribute to Chopin)

Nights clumped in despair and Eau de Vie
I toast to myself and to our anniversary, - it's October the 17th
but a different year, yet icy winds blow again, pasting stalactite grins
on the glass window pane- Chopin's chorale playing softly.

A leaf of Ballade No 1 in G Minor flutters,
its black serpentine notes recoiling, resigned
we share a commonality in cambered caskets as I refill
my glass mulling over shards of a life unlived at 39.

A repertoire of crested notes of a piano distilled
reflecting a discordant life so rapaciously unfulfilled.

Rise up now, conjure your feisty accented mazurka,
Obliquely interspersing diatonic pitches with chromatic scales
Stay a while, it's still night the menacing battle isn't lost yet
Ever so alive- I feel you pulse in my blue veins, I'm in love again.

PROSE POEMS:

CRIMSON HUES

Beyond the foliage, embroidered vistas
weave water hyacinths on silk with waves that
simmer in the glade like coffee in a cup, languishing
yet withdrawing to a lull. A gazelle bats its eyelids
feverishly on the landscape like the restless breeze
that wafts about the woodland.

Drops of dew pristine, reach out to drench
the opacity of paper roses. The blood petals of sun
reflect a spectrum through wrinkled substrates of winter
like rotifers struggling to breathe in brackish water. I am
the crimson hue of the petalled sun that drinks through
the chalice of icy winter, the drops throb in me- till eternity.

The dew drops simmer
Like crimson throbbing in veins
Wrinkled existence.

A FOOFARAW

The candle aflame turns into a recalcitrant dance of faltering breaths, the throbbing in my feverish head overpowers my senses. Time's hollow flute plays unabashed as my visit floods me with memories of Spain. Cravings of Cocaine fastened me in adamantine chains five years ago when my beauty was scarred under wheels of acrimony. Regular doses of Tobrol only amplified the manic depression.

An ocean thirsts
Life's arid footfalls to wash
A candle flickers.

Snowflakes of mind's nightfall melt away leaving a phlegmatic silence on puckered lips. Its frayed edges hurt the skin like brambles on a storm- tossed day. 'Somewhere my Love' jars in my ears, stinging them with deceit that lingers like an aftertaste in my mouth as I guzzle down Maraschino liqeur. The rawness of guilt haunts me as I succumb to the craving yet again. The candle burns out, wax melting away. This foofaraw in a capricious butterfly's life isn't so simple after all.

On a fresh green twig
A heron perches deftly
Wheel of death spins.

SUMMER ESCAPADES

Off the coastline of Limassol, salt soaks up the silver green of the sea. Epoxied hearts sway to a libidinous rhythm, clutching fire in their lidded eyes, gently releasing it as slivers of moonbeams. The charcoal night wears a pirate cape recklessly plundering elixir tingling from the nape of their necks.

A great white shark swirled in the coral reefs, stealing drippings from ventricles of the maiden's heart. Clavier strings of a song-bird echo the rain pattering on his window pane, enhancing the fragrance of white jasmine flowers that lie across her grave.

Now summer retreats into the throbbing breast of the southern hemisphere bludgeoned by the mistral to a deserted land. The pendulum of night swings incessantly to mark the solstice while errant waves of love will never return to the shore.

Lustful jasmine still
Hangs on their perfume kissed lips
Astral projection.

A WAR VETERAN'S STORY

In dust layered memorabilia, lie yesterdays crushed under unrelenting paperweights of unrest, forgotten. Restless fingers wrestle to free them but the grey lace curtains ward the wind off like an evil spirit. Tiny goblets sparkle on a veteran's military uniform reflecting silver hues of moon on sultry charcoal nights. He flings a pebble at the blue -blooded heart of an unforgiving azure, slicing a laden cloud like a coconut into two halves leaving its waters to flow and mingle with the earth where crimson roses grow nurtured by the blood of comrades.

War drapes itself in
Murky offshoots of hatred
Wine flows from goblets.

Regrets patter on his velvet lips like rain, his chest heavy with baggage resting upon the bridge of his delusions, awaiting a resolution. Diamonds bedecking the sky foretell the onset of another war- a cold war, in his mind. Weapons of hate have hardened his heart like iron bars that once held promises of love. Dawn jettisons a rainbow- there's hope on the other side.

Rain pelts from the sky
In a lark's trill
Impaling winter sleep.

THE MENAGERIE

Along the esplanade, a misty gloom loomed over denizens with green spiked leaves. The landau of night enveloped the cindered firmament with a sparkling veil akin to a bride. The rake she married, stole her heart in hollow promises etched out on tree barks. Her woes, a lizard's tail, sprouted again and again, each time she'd scrunch and toss them away into the sea of her misgivings.

She watched the menagerie of thoughts emblazon on window panes of her eyes, leering at her, each a split image of him. Love letters in the drawer of her desk lay crumpled in isolation for years like a squeezed- out lemon awaiting imminent death.

An alchemy of musings
Paint boats on canvas
Until storms erupt.

www.ingramcontent.com/pod-product-compliance
Lightning Source LLC
Chambersburg PA
CBHW051458130726
47987CB00005B/2373